IN CASE OF
BEARS

IN CASE OF BEARS

Poems by
PEGGY C. HALL

RILEY HALL
Miami, Florida

IN CASE OF BEARS
Poems by Peggy C. Hall

COPYRIGHT © 2006, PEGGY C. HALL.

"The Rubeariyat of Gus Greenbear" by SANDRA RILEY.

Cover painting *Stepping into a New Dimension* by BEVERLY FROST, reprinted with kind permission.

Book Design and Layout by JASON STOETZER.

A RILEY HALL publication. For more information, contact:

>RILEY HALL
>6501 SW 62ND COURT
>SOUTH MIAMI FL 33143
>
>rileyhall@gmail.com
>www.rileyhall.com

>ISBN 0-9665310-7-8

Library of Congress publication information available by request.

The rights of Peggy C. Hall to be identified as the author of this work are guaranteed under international laws. All rights reserved.

Printed in the USA.

Dedicated to

Sylvia Heller

and all my friends in Idaho

in loving memory of

Frank Heller

"The Man Who Sees Animals"

CONTENTS

PREFACE   9

IN CASE OF BEARS   13

    Facing the Bear   15
    It's Like …   16
    The Players at Silver Springs, Florida   18
    Getting Our Bearings   19
    In Case of Bears   20
    Ultrasoundings   24

IDAHO SUITE   27

    Idaho Second-Homecoming   29
    In Waste Places   33
    Idaho Morning   34
    Open Door, Early View   36
    More Birthday Power to You   37
    At an Arts and Crafts Show in Pierce, Idaho   38
    Paying Summer Respects   39
    For Sylvia, Our Spider Woman   40
    Sylvia's Prayer   41
    Frank's Prayer   42
    For Frank, the Man Who Sees Animals   43
    Sweatin' on the Fourth of July   44
    To Cody, Our Summer Dog   46
    Dreamcatcher Medicine   47
    An Epistle from Idaho to Maria, in Miami, Florida   49
    On Taking Chances in Idaho   50
    After the Fall   52
    On Big Cedar Road   53
    A Moment of Silence, Please   54
    Big Cedar, Idaho: 2 a.m.   55
    Idaho Metage   57

THE REST OF THE WEST — 61

The Rutting Season	63
A Madsong in Wyoming	64
An Old Feud	65
Calamity Jane's Lament	67
A Medicine Wheel Prayer	68
Hunters RV Park—Lakeview, Oregon	69
What We Saw in Spokane, Washington	70
Morning Tea with Mount St. Helens	72
Glass Beach, California	74
The Redwoods Reign	75
Home Sweet Coast	76

WILD THINGS — 79

Wild Things	81
An Alarum, or Thereby Hangs a Tale	82
Badgers and Bears	83
On Whiskey Creek	84
To Teddy Roosevelt	85
A Glose on Roethke's "In a Dark Time"	86
All Is Fair…	88
Irish, Indeed	89
Brother Bear	90
Dueling Bears	91
My Grandfather—Fred Clay Spradling	92
My Feelings Bared	93
Lullaby, My Baby Bear	94

YOU GOTTA HAVE ART — 97

On the Rocks	99
Photograph by Curtis: *Bear's Belly – Arikara (1908)*	101
Why Not?	103
A Wild Quadrille	104
Saturday Matinée	105
You Gotta Have Art	107
A Pantoum for Mark Runge	109
The Collection	110

CeleBEARations ... 113

- Antiphon, with Drums ... 114
- CeleBEARations ... 117
- My Birthday in Three-Steps ... 119
- In Praise Of ... 121
- The Mother Names of Bear ... 122
- Transamputation ... 123

And What about Our Teddy Bear? ... 125

- And What about Our Teddy Bear? ... 126
- A Madrigal by an Unnamed Bruin ... 127
- Lady Fern and the Three Green Bears ... 129
- The Rubeariyat of Gus Greenbear ... 140

Route 12, Idaho ... 145

- Route 12, Idaho ... 146

Acknowledgments ... 149

Index of Forms ... 150

PREFACE

WHY BEARS?

Like a bear, a poem is a strange animal: scary to approach, yet fascinating, drawing us to it by its exciting unpredictability and elusiveness, as we try to comprehend – yes, sometimes even to "capture"—it.

My fascination with bears began when I was researching and teaching Native - American literature, and read *The Secret Paw: The Bear in Nature, Myth, and Literature* by Paul Shepard and Barry Sanders. By the time I became serious about writing my own poems, I had made eight road trips to Kooskia, Idaho, where not only had I seen bear scat in the yard of our summer home, but also glimpsed bears living in the forest.

WHY "FORMS"?

To capture bear antics in words, I turned to Lewis Turco's *The New Book of Forms: A Handbook of Poetics*, which, to my delight, included examples of fiendishly complicated Irish and Welsh verse that appealed both to my unexplored heritage and to my quest for a new learning challenge after retiring from 30 years of teaching. As I worked through Turco's explanations of 300-plus international poetic forms A to Z (his list actually stops with W, for *wheel*) I attempted to follow his schematic diagrams and wise advice on the unusual forms: " . . . pay attention only to the rhyme scheme and syllabification." That was still a lot to pay attention to: for example, complex patterns of cross-rhymes within and between lines (not just the end of lines), or ending all Irish forms with the same first "syllable, word, or line with which it begins."

I was eager to write other equally interesting patterns, such as the Italian *canzone*, Malayan *pantoum*, and Norse *edda measures*. I wrote some easier, more familiar forms, such as acrostics, sonnets, *haiku* and spatial poems. However, I admit I began to flag by the time I reached Turco's Rs, so I encouraged Sandra Riley to write the Arabic *rubai* stanzas. "Let her celebrate her Lebanese heritage," I said.

"My Birthday in Three Steps," a silly bear poem that uses the *virelai* form, and "An Alarum, or Thereby Hangs a Tale," a *bob and wheel* about a surprising opossum, completed my self-imposed poetic mission. But there were and are some days that forms just wouldn't, couldn't and shouldn't cage the bear, or any other subject, and so they are only loosely bound – in free verse.

PEGGY C. HALL
MIAMI, FLORIDA
JANUARY 2006

The world has room to make a bear feel free-

The universe seems cramped to you and me.

-Robert Frost, *The Bear*

In Case of Bears

FACING THE BEAR

I sit at my desk, to get my bearings,
Westward Ho for the day.

You fix me, from your postered face.
Eye-level you glare, overbearing,
carrying me, clawing
but still crawling inward
past your brown, uncivil brow
and hidden teeth in calm-clenched mouth.
You wild one, eager for provocation,
I crouch in your quotidian cave.

I rest inside your sacred site

until you harry me out to write.

IT'S LIKE . . .
Kyrielle (French)

Roller coaster falling, twisting:
Hardly breathing—you gasp, exhale.
Brain and guts—you feel them listing—
Surprised by a bear on the trail.

Michael Jordan, towering, bending:
You a Shetland, he Clydesdale,
Eyed with awe and terror, blending,
Like greeting a bear on the trail.

Rocky Mountains, your newborn's smile:
Your fingers learning first words in Braille.
Chili peppers sear your throat while
Confronting a bear on the trail.

Past life scenes flash quickly, slowly:
A Greek valley of swallowtails.
Saved at six, baptized, and holy,
Good-byeing a bear on the trail.

Peggy C. Hall in Dixie, Idaho, 1992.

THE PLAYERS AT SILVER SPRINGS, FLORIDA
Cywydd Deuair Hirion (Welsh)

Fear is a powerful lure.
I went, prepared for torture,
dreaming cages, nightmare dogs,
trapped in the old analogues
between us, the bears and me.

There they played, no refugees
from bear pits or fairy tales,
but real bears, running pell-mell
to find peanut butter, fish
hidden by trainers. Impish
and clever, grizzly twins swam
with soft huffs, like dithyrambs
old, yet in time with Roy Clark
singing our country, his trademark.

There was a moat and a fence,
electrified, their province
where they played, not full grown,
Fed Ex'd bears from Yellowstone
Park. Mack flipped the bucket up
and water flowed like syrup
down his half submerged, tan coat.
Shyer Louie's own footnote
was tumbling down grassy plots
spacious and cool. The upshot
of my day at Silver Springs?
Bear play made fears seem nothings.

GETTING OUR BEARINGS
Ae Freislighe (Irish)

The bear fathers: Imitate
their courage. Sing their power
in your dancing. Integrate
spirited stance. Never cower.

The bear mothers: Comprehend
cave's life, winter's deep slumber
breathing, dreaming. Reverend
protectors. Berry hunger.

The bear cubs: Spring. Imagine
playful cuffings to prepare
sheathed copper claws. Medicine
lessons. Transform, like the bear.

IN CASE OF BEARS
Canzone (Italian)

Yellowstone Park—I can hardly bear
to contemplate each wild thing there: open range
for *carpe diem* buffaloes that bear
their heavy shawls like stocky Sherpa bear-
ers, that graze like glaciers in the moment
extended. But buffaloes can never be bears.
That statement can stand repeating, bear-
ing, as it does, on my state of mind,
or actually, being of many minds.
So, here goes: Buffaloes can never be bears.
Self evident, you claim. Not so. The wonder
is that not many people care to wonder

how categories tend to blunt the wonder
quotient of the animal, mammal named "bear."
Consider: Annie Sullivan was a wonder,
but she couldn't deflect bullets like Wonder
Woman. You think that's not a big enough range?
Do you remember the Seven Wonders
of the World? No pyramid is the wonder-
ous Great Wall of China. Think for a moment.
Science says the Big Bang was a moment
in time. Can our friend, Alice in Wonder-
land, snacking on mushrooms, get her mind
around the notion that it's all in her mind?

But there are other stories that are mind-
blowing. "Thaumaturgus" means a wonder-
worker, like Bishop Gregory, whose mind
moved a mountain. Was it because his mind-
set was on God, and saints must learn to bear
deflected praise, that he didn't lose his mind
but found a miracle? Let's call it mind
over matter, Greg as Power Ranger,
metaphysically using God's great range
finder to focus love. In my mind's
eye I see a matador at his moment
of truth: Will he make the kill? Moment-

ous only to those caught up in the moment,
carried away by the crowd's collective mind.
Where were you when Kennedy died? A moment
of silence, please. Imagine the moment
the sun first rose over Stonehenge. Wonder-
struck Druids making the most of the moment.
A moment is a moment is a moment?
So here we are, back to buffaloes and bears.
Aristotle knew how to think about bears:
As each one changes from moment to moment,
As each one grows and explores its ranges,
There is a constant we could call a range

light, like a guide for ships that are rang-
ing off course. This means, at any moment,
a channel to follow within the seas' ranges,
a "bearness" to follow, within forest ranges.
"Matter remains; form changes its mind."
Thus, when we discuss Himalayan ranges,
or Green Berets (who are not Texas Rangers),
or that pumpernickel cannot be Wonder
Bread, don't be surprised, don't even wonder
if I start to tear up, or hum "Home on the Range"
because I remember a small night-time bear
my son called Teddy. Little lost-time bear.

It is this quiddity we strive to bear
by climbing Pike's Peak, not a whole mountain range,
which becomes a decision of moment,
an act of will, as we meet our own minds.
Buffaloes can never be bears? I wonder.

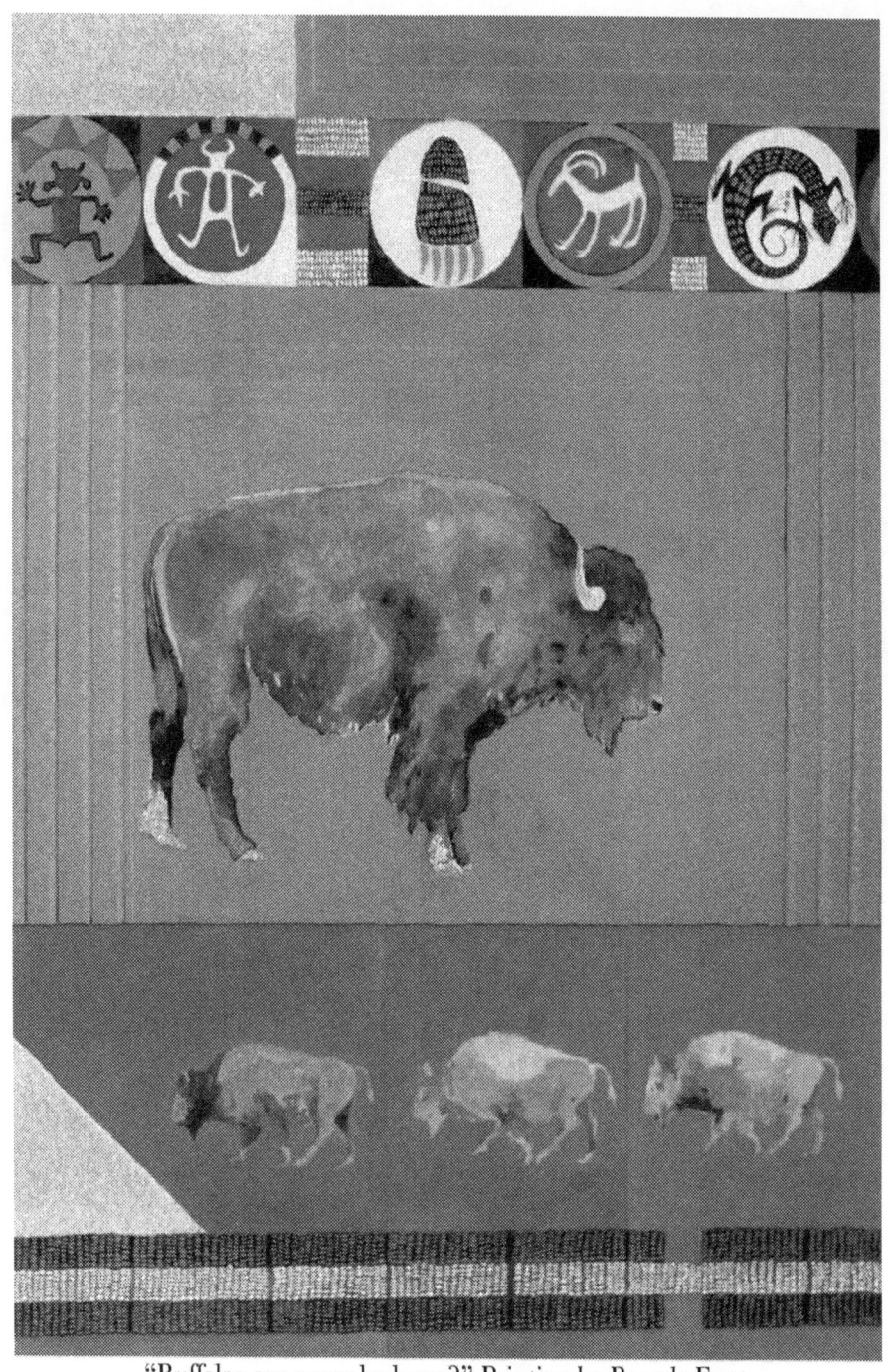
"Buffalos can never be bears?" Painting by Beverly Frost.

ULTRASOUNDINGS

It looks like . . .
sometimes a snail,
sometimes a fetus,
sometimes an eye
of hurricane,
whirlpool,
the bathroom drain.

She twists the knobs
and blood sing-songs,
breathing whales and seismic waves,
as blood flows around the clot
lodged in my artery,
like a new Airstream RV
trying to beat it out West.

Not that I ask to see or hear
the Frankenstein dials of ultrasound.
Not that I want to face the bear,
or see the maelstrom in his cave.

But there you are, my blood relation,
fixed on the screen,
big brown eye saying,
"Look at me!"

Stepping Into a New Dimension. Painting by Beverly Frost.

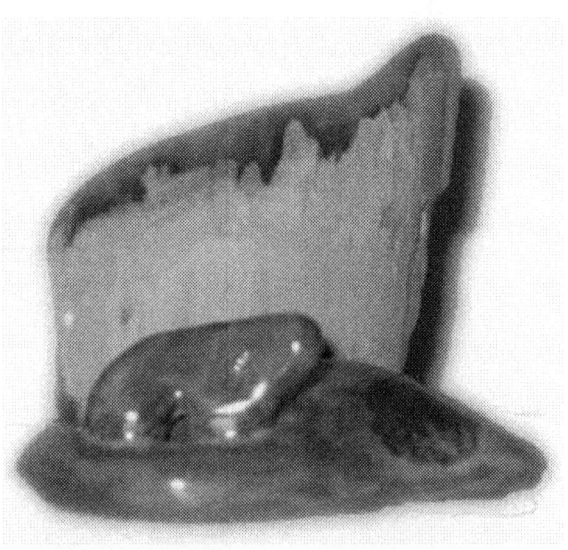

Idaho Suite

"And there is the ranch."

IDAHO SECOND-HOMECOMING

There is the trip west—
and there is the ranch,
and both are good, but different,
the same.

On Interstate 90, or 80, or 10,
corn high, corn low, being danced, being hoed,
we've seen the fields, a decade of roads.

But past and beyond the Badlands
or mesas,
looproads to monuments,
towers, and sights,
cow-town saloons, Wall Drug overnight,
detours to Death Valley
so hot in late June . . .

There is the ranch,
twelve miles up from town,
ten degrees cooler, or more in the shade.
We finally see deer, on Big Cedar Road,
white flowers high meadowed,
though the chicory's late,
Nez Perce Appaloosas
far down by the river.

Seems greener this year,
still raining like Spring,
at our ranch with two horses,
three cats, and three dogs,
who rush out to bark
then remember us
well.

"Appaloosas far down by the river."

"So what was this chicory we'd read of in books?"

IN WASTE PLACES

So what was this chicory we'd read of in books?
In books, somebody made coffee (the substitute kind),
In wars and depressions and other waste times,
With white roots roasted till dark brown and brittle,
Then ground and brewed and drunk from a pot.

And then we saw chicory for the very first time.
"Strikingly blue," said *Peterson's Guide*,
(Looked purple to us, who knew Bahama blues)
Light purple, or lavender royal robes.

Now, stiff naked stems salute us June mornings.
We meet them on roadsides (the *Guide*'s "waste places")
With their wild, wavy friends—the daisies—ox-eyed,
Or in our fresh meadow, uncut, near the drive.

Some run through our rockery, stalk by our ferns,
Square-tipped their petals, sun-opened toward nine,
Then close after noontime
(you have to be there to see them)

Or if clouds close them early,
They are whisked, through trickery, by tiny gypsies
Who take their fringed petals, to drape
Small shoulders too bare in waste places,
Too cool in the shade.

IDAHO MORNING
TRIVERSEN (AMERICAN)

The dogs escape early on,
      skimming up the chilly hill
            toward the salt lick for the deer.

Greedy Lucy Fatcat hefts
      her spots up on the cedar chest,
            chowing down Harleytom's grub.

In the brush the chickens cluck,
      happy to've picked the compost clean
            before the hawk swings their way.

Shadowcat hunkers in Syl's red roses,
      adding feathers—grosbeak gold—
            to his pile of petals.

Rochelle phones—wakes Frank's fish—
      "The moose is back and in our pond.
            Why not come and see?"

We take the toast—two cinnamons—
      to share next door
            with the neighborhood watch.

"The moose is back and in our pond."

OPEN DOOR, EARLY VIEW

Old pine-tree hill, crayon greens.

Chicory meadow, blue on blue.

Chicken combs like derricks pumping.

From my old yellow chair

With its raspberry stains,

'Cause I dip into berries

Like old-timey snuff.

MORE BIRTHDAY POWER TO YOU

Side-by "sister," my amazing Yankee friend,
Accept your name in poetry this Southerner has penned.
North and South, terse and wordy, yet as poles attract,
Drawn together, we have created a wondrous pact:
Rich in spiritual music, dramatic, intense,
A life of actions over words, we make it all make sense.

Ann is your middle name—and, you know, it's mine—
Never used, abjured by both, but good for acrostic rhyme.
Nonchalant, you drive the truck that hauls the firewood in,

Rescue injured hummingbirds, so gently, I can't imagine
Idaho trips without you, mountain prayers and quests,
Let alone our Florida garden, parrots, and the rest.
Entranced Flower Eagle, writing now of stones in clay,
You are beloved and valued on this, your special day.

Sandra Riley creates ceramic jewelry, set with semi-precious stones, fossils, beads, and pottery shards. She has written of her work in her book *Stone Poems/Wotai: Help on the Way*.

AT AN ARTS AND CRAFTS SHOW IN PIERCE, IDAHO

I want to ask, "Where are your teeth?"
although I know, already know,
having met you many times,
your hip-borne child
with chicken-bone breast and eyes that tear
as strangers stare
at mountain folk.

You drink in our wares, our artsy beads,
city pretties, priced and set
a world apart from well-drawn water,
old truck that drips as much and more
as blonde-nosed, stair-stepped, scruff-shoed kids,
whining quarters for a "pop."

Your man asks, "Whar y'all from?"
yet not believing me as I speak.
"Don't sound Kentucky t' me."
Rockies' man, though versed in tongues,
not hearing, no longer hearing,
far below my city patterns
the nasal vowels that thread our bones
through mountain chains across the land.

PAYING SUMMER RESPECTS

The day we saw her, Mrs. Skunk,
We chirped, "Oh look, a cute chipmunk!"
What did we know? (What's a grouse? That's a quail?)
We'd mainly trekked through city sales

Of Calvin's jeans (stone-washed, preshrunk).
But Frank, our guide, felt we'd be sunk
If, blundering on down this trail
We irked this mom. Matériel?

Reputed weapons, best used with spunk
To make us wish instead we'd quickly slunk
Away from babies on her tail.
Our leader whispered, "No bombshell

Should drop. She's not yet in a funk.
Stop! Be still. Become a trunk
Of cedar, a snail, a spent eggshell.
Quietly now, inhale, exhale."

Nonchalant. Unhurried stride. Punk
White stripes on her back. Like a monk
Apace, slow prayers for the Grail,
Or rather, Sister under veil,

Deigning to see if we would flunk
The test Frank's dogs often fail. (They'd stunk
Of musk, that odor so telltale
Only catsup could abate the smell.)

Three skunks strolled by, and when we'd drunk
The air pine-fresh, not full of gunk,
We hooted, stretched, hiked extra well
And thanked that small, august female.

FOR SYLVIA, OUR SPIDER WOMAN
Dizain (French)

You weave at your loom, glance up at them there,

hanging in corners, or draped on a plant.

The spiders all bless you, delighted to share

their secrets and skills, the myths that enchant

you, but not me, though beauty, I grant,

lies in the woof of the tales that are told

of Daddy Long Legs, Black Widow so bold,

of Ariadne, the Weird Sisters three.

Their stories enter your warp, threaded gold,

spider cloth made by loving devotee.

SYLVIA'S PRAYER

To thank you, God, I lay bare
The truths that Spider taught,
When I was young, made fresh aware
What Mother Earth had wrought.

She birthed the eggs from silken sacs,
Eight legs on each small frame,
For perfect balance front and back,
Renewed if one went lame.

I watched you, Spider, on my knees,
You spun both low and high,
You sidled down from Heaven's trees,
Connecting me to sky.

O Spider, wide-eyed, lacking lashes,
Did you see me there,
As you survived, stored flies in caches,
Inbound with silver hair?

Now, Great Spirit, stick my soul
Anew to webbed Earth's wheel,
Accept my praise as I extol
The patterns you reveal.

FRANK'S PRAYER
Cywydd Llosgyrnog (Welsh)

O great medicine wheel of life,

Marry me to a bearish wife.

When the knife of winter wind

Slashes spirit, slivers my heart,

She will gather me, piece by part

With loving art, safely denned.

FOR FRANK, THE MAN WHO SEES ANIMALS
Droighneach (Irish)

"Yesterday, two black bears, near Selway waterfall,

ran like all the Keystone Kops in matinees

I watched on Saturdays, before the basketball

game." So begins the tall tale (we suppose) he straightaway

tells. This is Frank, a forester, a wilderness

man, whose motionless stance means he can register –

with no fluster-nests, see newborns, or numberless

deer. Yes, Frank loves wild things, like wolves at Winchester.

With a faraway look, he speaks of a solitary

coyote pup, who pranced like an Astaire protégé

in front of his truck, then danced away, debonair.

"Coyote, two bears . . . . " He savors his yarns. "Yesterday . . ."

SWEATIN' ON THE 4TH OF JULY

The sweat lodge.

I "kept the door."
That is, I didn't go in,
but lifted tent blankets that closed your light,
and ushered you steaming into the night
when you had to emerge.

But mostly you stayed long, to pray.
Your voices I heard, but no exact words
sang on my left, as I watched by the door,
just fireworks and thunder, low on the right,
shhhh sounds in the meadow, high on our hill,
on the bench where the deer will lay down the grasses,

where you built all day, with the willows you gathered
close after dawn,
bending a frame, your lodge for the eight,
digging two fire pits, right for the rocks,
laughing and solemn, consulting Native books,
a circle of friends, close to the earth.

Black, white, yellow, and red.
I made the prayer ties, between twelve and two,
kitchen door open, July Fourth warm,
though it threatened to rain all day as you labored
to enclose the sweat lodge, to blanket and tarp,
to gather the rocks, to center the altar,
to string up the ties of yellow and white.

Dusk ready, you entered.
Then Frank placed the rocks,
poured water for steam,
and I closed the door
on your first round of four.

So I saw what you didn't
three hours and more,
as you prayed for us all, our darkness, our need:

Tall circle of cedars crossing the moon
that highlighted daisies, a deer field of flowers
that shone in the lightning, still miles away,
followed by fireworks
on neighbors' far hills
all, all on display for me, as
I kept the door.

TO CODY, OUR SUMMER DOG

I wish, just once, my son had

crawled onto my lap the way

you did each TV night, to settle

head and skinny front legs

into my side and pelvic bones.

That's all you fit, you needy dog,

with all your sighs and grinning gums,

your nudging, digging long black head,

stickers clinging to your ears,

silky

dusty

breathing face

content to settle

for my surrogate strokes.

DREAMCATCHER MEDICINE

Maria wove a catcher of dreams,
A web with healing hues,
A vine of sinew—supple, strong,
Beads green and cobalt blue.

Tiny stones from Mother Earth,
A shell from sea bed's art,
Maria fixed them all in air,
And fired them with her heart.

The catcher turns in each small breeze.
I watch it as I mend.
Its mobile balance, loving eye
Remind me of my friend.

Artist Maria Soliday.

AN EPISTLE FROM IDAHO TO MARIA, IN MIAMI, FLORIDA *

Dear Maria,

You want to know how our days are spent? We peruse beads.
We mix and match. Our bins and batches simply ooze beads.
From those we brought to ones we bought, we can't refuse beads.
They find us, in our van or on an ocean cruise. Beads
Made of glass, from stone and bone and clay. Dry bamboo beads
Are piled by African cowrie shells, native Sioux beads
Gained in trade, and Czech, Venetian, and Corfu beads.
In Prescott, Arizona's Bead Museum, we viewed beads
Amber crafted for pyramid builders, who accrued beads
For their spiritual power. The pharaohs valued beads.
But other cultures, from east to west, they all issued beads:
Attu whale tooth, Zulu tusk, yak bone Katmandu beads.
We love the odd ones: ostrich eggshells make ecru beads,
And ancient trees, fossilized wood, have become new beads.
In our travels, we've bought what's called I.O.U. beads—
Indian pawn, left long in the shop. We rescue beads,
And wonder, as we study each aged choker, whose beads
Were these? What life did they grace? Are they Veracruz beads?
We hunt for, we find, design, recreating art through beads.
Stringing a piece, our motto is: Have fun, do beads.

P.S. Am sending, UPS, a packet of Hindu beads.
Pray for us, as they do, with scripted, curlicue beads.

*Modeled on Jonathan Swift's satiric letter "An Epistle to Two Friends." The fun of an *epistle* (a *Didactics* form) lies in making the next-to-last word in each line rhyme, while keeping the focus on the main subject of the poem, the last word. In Swift's poem, the focus word is "sick," which he uses 33 times.

ON TAKING CHANCES IN IDAHO
Standard Habbie (Scottish)

We've bid at quite posh silent auctions,
And at cheap ones—PTA collections.
We have a true predilection
For raffles of all kinds,
Whether charitable confections,
Or those less refined,

As viewed, that is, by society's
Lights. We snuff our sensibilities
And drop our East coast priorities
The further we go West.
We take a chance on oddities
Most famous or obscurest.

One contest in particular,
(Though no prize was vehicular,
And there was nothing cellular)
Lured us to buy tickets
For twenty-seven prizes, singular
Stuff, ranging from trinkets

To the top prize: a chain saw (or cash).
Other goods to win were a flash-
Light (3-cell); a cargo bag for stash;
An emergency road kit;
A Stanley thermos for the dash;
A cord of firewood, split;

A sweatshirt; a hairpin lace afghan;
A camping chair; a tool kit and lantern;
Tasco scopes for the rifleman.
But what did we want to win the most?
That appealed to us, Idaho suburban?

A truck load (delivered) of ripe compost.

AFTER THE FALL

Startled hooves kicked free from ground to sky. The fawn,
as if to spark a dampened match, quick-scratched
the phosphorous mist that seemed a frosted lawn,
but proved no purchase firm. She fell. Detached,
I watched my dog stop short, ravine below
morn-filled with fog, his barks the hollow sound
that rocky earth drums back to wake our slow
and sleepy eyes, our careless ears. Around
the gorge I tacked to find a way downhill
without the dog, dreading what I knew lay there,
a limp and flat, becalmèd sail. I well
remember my regret and my despair.
But then, before my touch or sigh, she rose.
Though stunned, she ran, alive, into the forest close.

ON BIG CEDAR ROAD

Oh! ye'll take the high road and I'll take the low road . . .
- Old Scotch Air

    We walked the high road
    above the middle mist
    which friezed tall trees
    that bulked the bank
    of stream below our feet

    and glimpsed, as though our
    rain hoods framed them so,
    startled deer, in Monet light
    (subtly washed blues and greens)
    poised for flight

A MOMENT OF SILENCE, PLEASE

If I could be a deer
a sixty-seconds deer
I could look down
from my hill
of haunch-high
brush

pause each hoof
still both ears and eyes
wait out the legged shapes

that halt below, arrested blurs
that soon move on
as I must do
with leaps
and bounds

BIG CEDAR, IDAHO: 2 A.M.

Startled awake, the deer

thrashed the grasses,

rushing from their heavy rest

not very far from the opened door

surprising me

who expected

only sleepless stars.

"Twelve Sandys cloned to climb …"

IDAHO METAGE*

I measure the barn
by Sandy's height
five feet small

and laugh to picture
twelve Sandys
cloned to climb

up 60 feet
while Mel drawls
its history out

about a boy
at eighteen
designing, building big

wide roof (beacon
seen for miles)
a prodigious space

Mel employed
as shop and palace
for King and Prince

*measurement by size or volume

two Belgians drafted for fun rides
no hay, just cart for
us, and grandkids

who collected jumbo eggs
from Mel's "chicken condo"
not crowded

by cows, plows, dogs, cats,
and children
in the barn's vast vault

they loved the lambing
in the heated stalls
bitter wooly winters

but couldn't fathom
why we gathered here
40 strong, to drum and keen

that endless
August eighth
our Frankie died.

"Two Belgians drafted for fun rides."

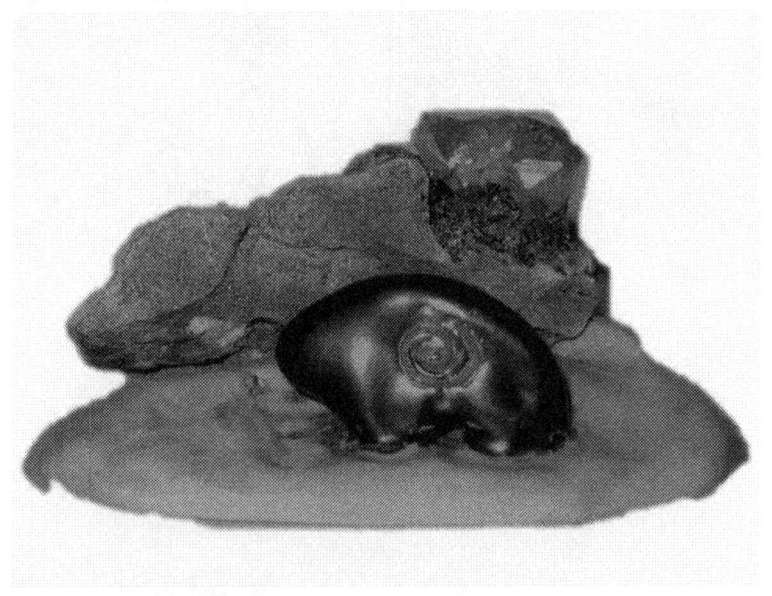

The Rest of the West

THE RUTTING SEASON

More coffee, please.
You know that tour that shows you the tracks

Left by wagons going West?
Is it Oregon or Santa
Fe?
Exciting stuff if you're . . .

More coffee, please.
Yes, we've seen the

Corn Palace, eight or nine times now.
Honey, what was the mural theme last year?
Oh, one panel showed locusts—the seven-year kind—
In the rows of corn—imagine, a picture
Created with shucks and husks and cobs and
Everything related to . . .

More coffee, please.
Yes, we have our favorite

Routes, and RV parks, from Florida to Idaho; then south to
Utah on I-15, oh, we like the heat
Though it does excite her heart
Sometimes.

A MADSONG IN WYOMING

Across this stream we pass, we pass,
the roadway ribbons in
meandered pain and knotted loops.
Where did it all begin?
I've come so far for zero miles
related to some kin.

God! Crazy Woman Creek again
not sleeping in its bed—
They woke her up to make her rest,
cut off her toes, then said,
"Let's take a leg to make her whole."
Paralyzed, I quickly fled.

Oh, Tom and Jane could sing this song
and join our choir of one,
we who've found and lost the way
to Crazy Woman run,
where tuning out is screaming in—
an end that's just begun.

AN OLD FEUD
Elegiacs (Greek)

In Memory Of Matthew Shepard

"Brutal assault in Wyoming," where cowboys, for cattlemen, punch cows,
Brand them with signs, with their hot seals. So the newspaper said.

Arabic, German—the victim knew these, but he pleaded in U.S.,
Begged them in English to please stop with their fists, with their burns.
Hung on a deer fence, he "looked like a scarecrow," said bikers who found him,
Nervously telling their blunt brush with the hate in this crime.

"Martyrdom," "transformed" are words in the article, pitiful cop-outs,
License for round-ups, for pogroms of the Jews or the gays.

"Shepard," the registrar read at his dorm, where his father also lived once,
Passed on his legacy, he thought, to his gentle, sweet son.

Greenbear Chronicles' author Sandra Riley at Calamity Jane's grave.

CALAMITY JANE'S LAMENT*

Folks said I wailed—for sure, that ain't true,
I was too busy, his blood on my arm—
My teeth were rippin' his shirt into strips
To tie up my Bill, his sweet face still warm.

One said I stole . . . Oh damn, how he lied!
Why would I pilfer Wild Bill's gold dust pouch,
When all that I wanted was my gold charm
That lay with the nuggets, worn from his touch?

His new wife said I "departed from truth."
She rode, so dainty, from Bill's Boot Hill grave.
But I knew he'd called me his "Bullwhackin' Bird,"
And loved his Canary, who couldn't behave.

But mostly who lied was murderin' McCall,
Who left Hickok dyin' on the bar floor.
Jack said he saw me pick up Wild Bill's cards,
Aces and eights, as he ran out the door.

McCall said I was drunk, or too yeller to shoot,
The truth is much tougher, damned hard to tell:
My anger at Bill for turnin' his back
Blinded my aim—and put me in hell.

*Martha Jane Canary Burke (1852-1903) was a famous frontier markswoman, whose name was often linked to James Butler "Wild Bill" Hickok. He was buried in the cemetery at Deadwood, South Dakota after his untimely death.

A MEDICINE WHEEL PRAYER

I stand before the stones in prayer,
in easy morning or hard-stormed night.
Enclosing, curling smoke around me
readies my prayer, steadies me groundward,
wisps me skyhooked, lifts me up,
sage-sense quickened, to learn the birds.

Help me see their unheard songs
that beat their way over water,
my path today through mind and matter,
sense and soul.

School me towards a loving heart.

HUNTERS RV PARK – LAKEVIEW, OREGON

Our headlights attacked the long dark drive
flanked by ponds on each shadowed side.
Then Sandy stopped, surprised.

Deployed across the narrow bridge
crowded together, in close rank file,
geese barred our way to night's bed and board.

The van inched slowly forward, as through the waves,
but the sea never parted
even when we honked.

Instead, the gaggle began to trumpet,
pressed closer, wings attentive,
and breasty fronts proud.

No lone eagles here, they moved in formation
save one odd bird with Canadian stripes.

Was he a fifth columnist? Reluctant draftee?
No, quickly he joined them, this troop with *esprit*.

Our quick-thinking chief called for stale crackers
which we threw from the windows
with chilling war whoops.

Decoyed from their places, the enemy fled,
goose-stepping in rhythm that let us now pass.

Checked in for the night, we laughed in triumph . . .
until the clerk showed us where our hookup lay:
Across the bridge and back through the squadron.

WHAT WE SAW IN SPOKANE, WASHINGTON

Skybows—white—jetters' trails
hook to Earth on either side
to handle well a stewpot summer.

Bridges—crescents—city crowns
vault above descending Falls.
They watch the river genuflect.

Fishing pole parabolas
throw their anchors from the banks,
and string our eyes upon their lines.

"They watch the river genuflect."

MORNING TEA WITH MOUNT ST. HELENS

I burn my lips. Again. Your snowcapped, pre-blown, pretty face preens on my cup, like simper-sister Fujisama. Façades. I scorch my tongue, never having learned the peace of patience; erupting rather more than less, quicker than most. I muse how the potter, still surprised five years past that May, sang to us of how he'd scooped your ashes, ashes removed a state away from tremored earth, but Idaho close to darkened sun: *"I wasn't thinking urns at all, but of a glaze to make the colors 'pop,' the white blues bleeding south, over brown and raven black. Ashes for the underglaze. A pinch a batch. And look, see the other side? Rich mud flow seeping down from the rim. Bottom's inscribed, 'Mt. Saint Helens Volcanic Ash.' Every piece."* I singe my nose, steam still rising from the blend I have brewed in your recovered bones.

"Morning tea with Mount St. Helens."

GLASS BEACH, CALIFORNIA

We are here early, fatigued but greedy.
Fogged coast, low-tide beach, sea-weedy cove.
Grey gulls that yap from craggy giant rocks
remind me of puppies on this cold day.

Sylvia stoops and scans oh so carefully,
yellow hair on turquoise jacket.
She finds the "finds" and has an eye
for fused, knobby, ocean-scoured shards.

Sandy scoops millioned bitty pieces, two
buckets full of Fort Bragg's past.
A hundred years lie at our feet, dishes and
glasses and bottles dumped on the sand.

I rest high above to watch the two play,
as waves work to grind and polish
all these discards,

and ready new goods
for Nature's shore store.

THE REDWOODS REIGN
Haiku

trees shower shadows—

down they flow to forest floor

up rise our spirits

HOME SWEET COAST

Yep, been out West—more times than ten,
Seen hunks of mountains, some rodeoed men,
Kiss-assed dust on graveled roads, when
Summer finally dried up spit.

So maybe I did see more stars,
And (what I liked most) fewer cars,
Felt barroom fire from chapped guitars
Strummed to warm my East Coast heart.

Nope, still don't want to move,
Just love it, leave it, as I prove,
A needle fits a certain groove—
No CD cowboys need apply.

Wild Things

WILD THINGS

I preferred them cut
Long stems in crystal vases
Flowers arranged

Or corsaged for proms,
Only orchids, with streamer ribbons
That brushed my breasts as I danced

But now it is the oddest thing
Since Maria sent the wild-flower card
(16 varieties in 100 seeds)

I tear the card up over the garden
To scatter small parts
Littering wide and deep and free

AN ALARUM, OR THEREBY HANGS A TALE
Bob and Wheel (English)

YOU SCRABBLED UP THE SCREEN ON OUR DOOR
And startled us blinking from our dreams.
Ten clawed toes scribbling soft tracks,
Like a monk in his still scriptorium
Testifying that the dead live again
                like you:
           rising, slowly and in stealth
           as rebels make their *coup
           d'état* on the Commonwealth,
           overturning, to begin anew.

YOUR STOUT BODY BLOTTED OUT THE MOON
Swung suspended like Spiderman's twin
Like mural scarab in an Egyptian tomb
Or worse, in a bat's vertical stance,
You posed, feigning Death himself,
                and froze
           as a coffined vampire could
           before he woke and rose
           to haunt the neighborhood
           and victims that he chose.

OUR DRAMATIC LIGHTS—THEN YOUR HEROIC DASH
Told us the truth of your playacting ploys.
Fifteen babies on your back, of nearly black fur
Like peas from your pouch, pointy white faces,
Like humanoid pods for alien births.
                O Possum,
           a Bodysnatcher? Not your trick.
           But there is a conundrum:
           How can you be so quick
           when you are post-mortem?

BADGERS AND BEARS
Rhupunt (Welsh)

Come, trace the signs:
Burrow designs,
clawed-tree guidelines—
learn well their strength.

Watch Badger's will:
She defends hills,
braves foes until
dead, or claws sheathed.

And Bear stands tall,
claws shaped to maul
rivals or brawl
to any length.

Smaller, larger,
they fight dangers.
Bears and Badgers—
take on their strength.

ON WHISKEY CREEK
Englyn Unodl Crwca (Welsh)

Banff, Alberta (AP)—Park wardens Thursday shot and killed the grizzly bear they think is responsible for three attacks on humans, one of them fatal, less than a kilometre from the town in the last 10 days.
                                           -Vancouver Province Sept. 4, 1980.

They came fishing in my creek
each time I would go to seek
slippery swimmers, so sleek on each side,
wide-eyed fish I made weak

and bloody, mauled with sharp claws,
ripping teeth, my hungry jaws.
Why would I leave just because humans came
and named us bears as outlaws?

When four intruded on my space,
a willowed pond, special place
with forest close, I gave chase, knocked down two.
I slew one, bit his face.

Beavers were building that day.
Two men strode by the stream. They
were surprised, when one, halfway up a branch,
was wrenched down straightaway.

He struggled like badgers do,
then lay quiet when I threw
him on the bank. I withdrew into the brush
so lush, only home I knew.

TO TEDDY ROOSEVELT
Rionnaird Tri-Nard (Irish)

Bear-brash, bold hunter

Too eager, ego rash.

The blood-rush of ambush—

Your brush with Death, Bear-Brash.

A GLOSE ON ROETHKE'S "IN A DARK TIME"*
Glose (Spanish & Portuguese)

Roused from sleep, startled by the raven,
I hear him and smell him. The squirrels disagree
On distance in the dusk. Then, opened, even
IN A DARK TIME, THE EYE BEGINS TO SEE

His head and arms, a shape against the sky screen,
Similar burly bearish form. He makes
Motions that tell me I have been seen.
I MEET MY SHADOW IN THE DEEPENING SHADE,

But even as he scrambles, his mouth is dumb.
Cubs lie silent on the leaves. I smell their blood,
And hoarsely bellow that revenge come.
I HEAR MY ECHO IN THE ECHOING WOOD.

Quick to the cedars. He climbs so high that
I cannot follow. He listens to me
Lowly growl, heartily roar. He stares at
A LORD OF NATURE WEEPING TO A TREE.

This tree already knows my claws, the mark
I've stretched tall to scratch again and again,
And I see where my back has broken the bark.
I LIVE BETWEEN THE HERON AND THE WREN,

All meadows and streams I fully explore,
Browsing through seasons, avoiding men.
This is my home range, once a lush space for
BEASTS OF THE HILL AND SERPENTS OF THE DEN.

The man rips off limbs, as if to smooth
This trunk into birch, but I know his goal
Is to drive me away. Which of us has proven
WHAT'S MADNESS? BUT NOBILITY OF SOUL

Is a mystery that lives in between
Day and night, awaiting the clash of desire
And fate. What creature's intent has not been
AT ODDS WITH CIRCUMSTANCE? THE DAY'S ON FIRE

Behind my eyes, as I rage to overcome
His scent, his being that killed the pair
I sired. I beat the dank ground like a drum.
I KNOW THE PURITY OF PURE DESPAIR.

I hear the crying of the lynx, the bat
Wings flapping past in the light rainfall.
I drink the grass blades, look up to see, flat,
MY SHADOW PINNED AGAINST A SWEATING WALL.

I rest. I wait. But though there is no spark
Of sun for him to see, I hear him brave
A free descent. I pick out a landmark—
THAT PLACE AMONG THE ROCKS. IS IT A CAVE

I will drag him to? And what before
That? Blows and rending? What flesh will I save?
Will he finally lie on the lakeshore
OR WINDING PATH? THE EDGE IS WHAT I HAVE.

*Read just the final lines of each stanza for Theodore Roethke's original poem, told from the human's viewpoint.

ALL IS FAIR . . .
Cyrch A Chwta (Welsh)

No bears make wars, but if they
did, there would be no mêlée
as in Homer, Hemingway,
or the latest matinée
with space weapons that display
world-breaking power, doomsday
battles, romantic rewards.
No bear hordes would act that way.

But one bear, with cubs in tow,
would not hesitate to show
berserker rage. The deathblow
might be swift, or could be slow
and crushing, from this Sumo
wrestler. With her huge torso,
hugging arms and armored eyes,
war bear tries to stop her foe.

IRISH, INDEED
Rannaigheacht Mhór(Irish)

Bear tales told in Dublin town

tend to be downed with dark gold

ales, then spit straight out, thrown

about gemstoned ears—raw, ribald.

Wryly, women grin. Cheeks blush—

a rush of Celtic cinnabars.

Though there's blarney, balderdash,

lasses love these brash, boorish bears.

BROTHER BEAR
Séadna (Irish)

Claws bite, teeth click, throat breathes chaos:

The "other's" red rage. He awes

me, draws blood. Unnerved, I observe

the cruel curve of his claws.

DUELING BEARS

        The lips stretch taut
         I see the gums
         of mouth ajar
         ready to growl
       from slanted throat
         uplifted nose
     eyes luminous, widely
        threaten, glint
with each whip of the head
that seems to fill the space
          I breathe:

My	Myself
mother	in the mirror
in one of her moods.	in one of my moods.

MY GRANDFATHER – FRED CLAY SPRADLING
Clogyrnach (Welsh)

Grandmother married a bear. Gruff
Black Irish ordering, "Enough!"
when three child cubs fought,
for Fred Spradling taught
(as he thought), Real Life stuff:

Surviving Great Depression days,
hustling grub, finding jobs that staved
off death, even when
that meant the mines, men
burying kin, coalfield wages.

But each spring saw Fred Clay emerge
from worksleep cave. He was the scourge.
Feuding mountain schemer.
Rival baseball teams,
winning dreams on the verge.

To celebrate, he home made wine,
elderberry, not much refined,
that ran from his mouth,
dripped pawward, uncouth.
Fred Bear's way, all ursine.

MY FEELINGS BARED

I need to fatten on thimbleberries and grubs
pass day's hours in blowy meadow crossings
scratch my back forever on trees
snuffle up the scent of winter's new cave

I want to fish in the pools
of notime, nolimit
or contemplate my claws
and cuff the cubs—as mother bears do.

Instead

I am baited by expectant, dutiful dogs
that yap and harry
just one more jig
O funny bruin
backed to the wall

Shall I grin and bear it?
Growl for one last smoke?

Or just bare my carnivores
and chew them all up
into gobbets?

LULLABY, MY BABY BEAR
Deibhidhe (Irish)

Lullaby, my baby bear,

honey dreams hang everywhere,

sticky paws, press to my breast,

rest, succumb to sleep's conquest.

Cub-sister's slain, by my mate.

Her death I must validate,

keep you dry and safe, so I

croon and cry love's lullaby.

Maria Soliday stands by her art.

You Gotta Have Art

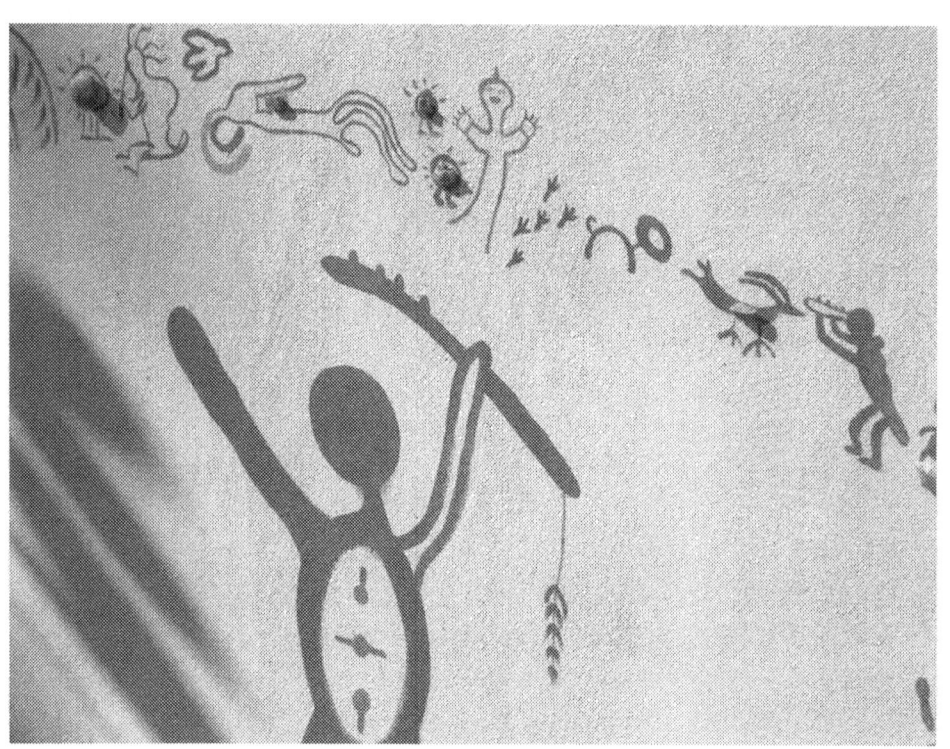

Mural by Maria Soliday.

ON THE ROCKS
Cyhydedd Naw Ban (Welsh)

Douse the torch and close the cave! Bears must
sleep the winter's moons away, till crust
breaks and rivulets flow in their quest
to the sea. First, you laugh as I wrest
the light from your hand, then you protest
the public must gaze at the best
petroglyph bears in Norway's caves, cast
between hunters' spears, among the vast
number of beasts painted in the past.

You label me an iconoclast.
What I am is a poet-artist
who still feels their power. I resist –
as lines fade and bear paws are lost
from the world, at myth-dying cost.

Bear's Belly – Arikara (1908). Photo by Edward S. Curtis.

PHOTOGRAPH BY CURTIS: BEAR'S BELLY – ARIKARA (1908)

Heart-mysteries there ...
                              -Yeats

Red man—a sepia man—stands inside the brown bearskin.
Cinnamon-brown, skyward-snouted, gut-split grizzlyskin
       enrounds a solemn face.
Wide fur shoulders loose snug a broad chest,
papoose-style for the camera's cradleboard pose.

           *"I call to the mysterious one who yet
       Shall walk the wet sands by the edge of the stream
       And look most like me, being indeed my double ..."*

Paleface Mr. Curtis stood a tripod before brown bearman,
       focused on this dancer, stilled Ree dancer
who hid "elk horns" of hair (Arickaree means "horns")
    but bared his breast scars, sun-drawn cicatrix
           for the lensman's unsparing gaze.

       Hanging dead on my wide high wall
your *wa rooh teh*, medicine mystery, breathes strong.
Light glints off forehead, noseridge, chin, and ribs,
       vertical light that splits your body
       as it meets your arms, uplifted bruin arms
           in photo axis for Edward Curtis.

           *"O body swayed to music, O brightening glance,
           How can we know the dancer from the dance?"*

"Bear's Belly"—is that your name?
Your place in every mythos of whale, womb, well or tree?
What *koo nooghke*, bear encounters, brought you to this stance
with one strange clouded, injured eye oracular, cast askance?
Lean swimmer muscles show you could have killed a fishing bear.
Your tribe is noted so.
Or is your cloak a farmer's trade?
Are you a shaman, chief, or priest
robe-gifted by your dancing clan?
Or healer bear, transformed to man?

After the wait, the shutter's closure, did you bow your bearmasked head?
Lower spirit helper's sky-sniffing face?
Return to earth-loving steps that praised survival of your small-poxed people,
Dakota-war wasted but never extinct?
What circle rhythms entranced you when Mr. Curtis packed up his gear?

*"From ruin or from ancient trees,
For I would ask a question of them all."*

You hang alive on my wide high wall,
mystery man in waist-high pose, with no feathers, beaded strings,
not even feet in moccasins painted blue like cigar-store Indians, circa 1908.

I want to tell you what I see:
Time clad, rite scarred, shadowed bare body
embraced by cave mother's winter fur
emerging toward the sun
from your twin brother's sleep.

*"When two close kindred meet,
What better than call a dance?"*

WHY NOT?

      2
There a cub
rested wetly
on the road

1
By Route 12
non-linear
runs a river

          3
Black furred rear
bolting in
bolero twirl

    4
as if to
entertain
us

      5
as the bear
went over
the mountain

A WILD QUADRILLE
Byr A Thoddaid (Welsh)

She who becomes a bear in the bear-dance
For a brief while can speak for the bear.
— Shepard and Sanders, *The Sacred Paw*

Spring thunder drummed awake, we three
watch our mother two-step with trees,
lift her paw palms to sun rays cure,
cuing cubs how power's won.

Summer tumbles, overturning
rocks and rolling, young ones learning.
Sixth year *pas de deux* we mate, males fight,
foxtrot and procreate.

Fall hoedown, felling acorns from red oaks,
orgy of fruit, wild plum.
We swing to kill, in Nature's round
before our fat sleep, underground.

Winter dens we find, or rooms carve out,
cradling cubs we unwomb.
Dream of two-leggeds, drums and rites
that rasp us out to dance in the light.

SATURDAY MATINÉE
Sneadhbhairdne (Irish)

Gentle Ben. Remember gangly
Legs? Lips, dental,
Giggle bared? No bear more civil
Than Ben, Gentle?

Mural by Maria Soliday.

YOU GOTTA HAVE ART
Cyhydedd Hir (Welsh)

Mural painting day.

Maria says, "Stay
and watch the bear weigh
in." Zuni bear,
looking west, not east,
outlined in a frieze
of fish, birds, and beasts,
rounded back, large ear.

I love them, big and
small, in sea, air, land,
but I understand
Bear most. His heft
of mind, spirit strength
that stretches full length
his heartline, wavelength
that brings his gift.

Gus Greenbear poses with artist Mark Runge's *Moses & the Twelve Tribes of Israel.*

A PANTOUM FOR MARK RUNGE
Pantoum (Malayan)

I say, Mark, is this about you, or art, or Gus?
We circle the walls, admiring your dogs and ducks,
Then stop, blinded, as on the road to Damascus,
Before your piece called "Moses." We're thunderstruck.

Others circle the walls, admiring your dogs and ducks.
They read your credo: "Anything that processes has a life."
They reach your piece called "Moses." They're thunderstruck.
A teddy bear as Moses? Does this verify

Your vision, credo, "Anything that processes has a life?"
Are the ducks in the wagon the twelve tribes of man?
Our Gus bear as Moses? Does this, too, verify
"There is no such thing as low art," your last *koan*?

The ducks in his wagon are the twelve tribes of man.
We stop, enlightened, as on the road to Damascus.
"There is no such thing as low art," laughs your *koan*.
I say, Mark, this is about you, and art, and Gus.

THE COLLECTION
Awdl Gywydd (Welsh)

Made of stone, cloth, paper, clay,
Bears array my shelves and walls.
Hang, in silver, from my neck,
Holidays, bedeck my halls.

Medicine-wheel bear-totem,
(Turquoise gem), helps me to heal,
Prompts strong songs of coral eyes,
Vivifies my idling will.

Carved from redwood, "Shorty" dreams
Western streams, or honeycomb.
"Bear's Belly" picture nearby:
Man occupies brown-skin home.

Onyx bears support my books,
Sturdy looks on bruin faces.
Ceramic mother nurses cubs,
Gives them rubs in itchy places.

Benbow Inn and Bridge of Bears –
Places rare, charmed keepsake thoughts:
Plump teddies on antique chairs,
Gulf-spanning bears, gold inwrought.

Which was my favorite bear?
Acting unaware, the one
Scampering across the road
In wild coat of cinnamon.

The collection, in hand-carved cabinet by Beverly Frost.

Photo by Frank Wendeln.

CeleBEARations

ANTIPHON, WITH DRUMS*
Antiphon (Liturgical)

Chorus: We celebrate, with sounding drums . . .
                [repeat line as desired]

Versicle: She swims inside the Cosmic Womb,
                Encircled by both dark and light,
                Through air and water, and in fire
                Our Mother Earth is born tonight.

Chorus: We celebrate, with sounding drums, the O . . .

Versicle: And on Her moves the first-born man.
                He loves the sun, its spirit whole,
                Sun essence, Center, Principal,
                An image of the Oversoul.

Chorus: We celebrate, with sounding drums, the One . . .

Versicle: Spirit, delighted, gifts him woman,
                Offers balance, shadows to cool,
                Twofold strength to bear the future,
                Practice for his theories, tools.

Chorus: We celebrate, with sounding drums, the Two . . .

Versicle:	Beginning, middle, and an end—
	So goes life's story, moves the moon,
	Raises spires, triangle forms,
	Rears us all, in Earth's commune.
Chorus:	We celebrate, with sounding drums, the Three ...
Versicle:	Where seasons, winds, directions rule,
	They ground us, measure space and time,
	So on our watch, always in awe,
	We praise the ordered, Great Sublime.
Chorus:	We celebrate, with sounding drums, the Four ...
Versicle:	We swim inside the Cosmic Womb,
	Encircled by both dark and light,
	Through air and water, even fire
	We are born, are born tonight.
Chorus:	We celebrate, with sounding drums, the All ...

*An antiphon is a liturgical "dialogue between choirs, one choir singing the *versicle*, the other singing the response (Turco)." My performance piece begins with one drummer, who creates his/her own rhythm. Principal speakers/chorus/drummers are then introduced, stanza by stanza. As each drummer joins in with a new rhythm, the work should increase in scope, pace, and intensity.

Sandra Riley, Peggy C. Hall, Gus Greenbear & a friend *celeBEARate The Greenbear Chronicles.*

CELEBEARATIONS
Hir A Thoddaid (Welsh)

"In Silesia, Hungary, and Carinthia, the feast of Candlemas (February 2) is still called Bear's Day, and on that day the bear emerges from his den, the belief goes, to discover whether or not he has cast a shadow."
— Shepard and Sanders, *The Sacred Paw*

Our forebears knew that bears were kin.
Once a woman married a bear, then
The Bear Mother bore us, to begin
a special race, half divine, bearskin
dressed, part human, nakedly bold and brave.
Altars in caves hold bones of our twins.

Eons before any fireworks show,
the night was lit by Great Bear's glow:
Four-starred bear pursued by seven foes,
finally caught before winter's snow,
but always patterned lights to guide the way.
Travelers worldwide bless this sky fresco.

There is a festival where men slay
the revered bear, in ritual ways,
to remind them winter does not stay.
In spring the bear's emergence portrays
return, rebirth. Through men they flow, and bears—
Ancient days, holy days, holidays.

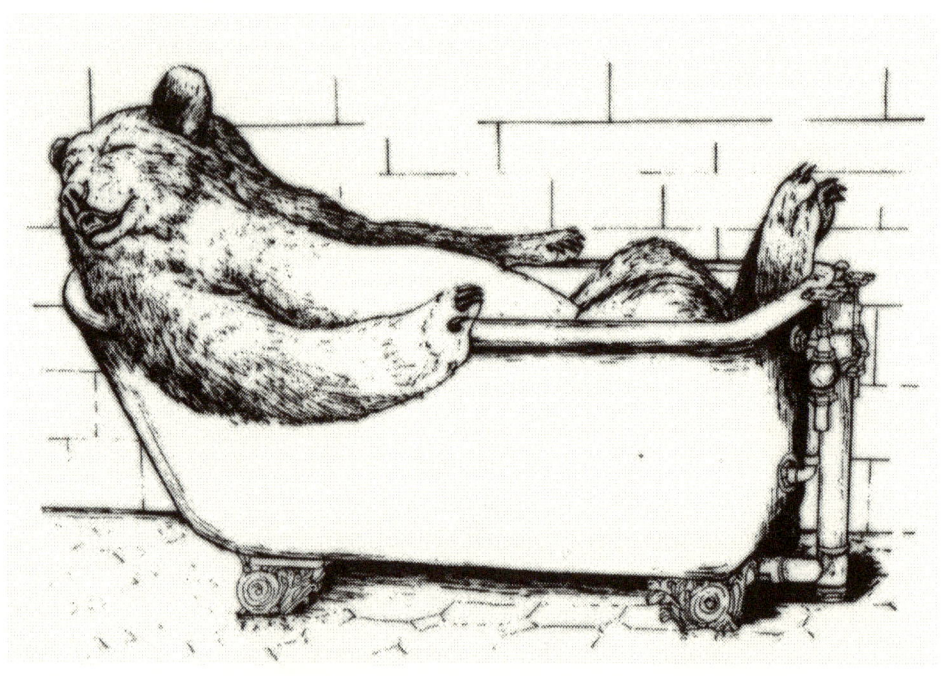

Saturday Night. Ink drawing by Beverly Frost.

MY BIRTHDAY IN THREE-STEPS
LAI (FRENCH)

On this, my birthday
At the Bear Café
We will
Drink café au lait,
Sample the buffet
Until
We hear the deejay
Turn up the sound, play
Nashville!

LAI NOUVEAU

On this my birthday
At the Bear Café
We will
Drink café au lait,
Sample the buffet
Until
We hear the deejay
Turn up the sound, play
Pop, rock, and reggae
Uh uh, no ballet!
Merry
We'll sing loud and sway
Dance our best bear way
Hairy
Latin *merengue*.
On this, my birthday
We'll pause, eat pâté
And have an entrée
That smells
Like fish, a gourmet
Tuna, or sunray
That swells
My belly okay
At the Bear Café

We'll eat (last) parfait
With nuts on the tray,
Then head
To a matinée.
No, we cannot stay.
We fed
At the Bear Café
On this, my birthday.

VIRELAI

On this, my birthday
At the Bear Café
We will
Drink café au lait,
Sample the buffet
Until
We hear the deejay
Turn up the sound, play
Nashville!
We'll bear-dance with skill,
Get our line-dance fill
Bears know
How to show good will,
How to do the drill:
Elbow
Room you must fulfill
Not to take a spill
Or blow.
Follow the tempo
Not too fast or slow
Olé!
After the demo,
Going with the flow,
We'll lay
Our heads down, although
Some treats we'll forego
Today.

IN PRAISE OF

A beach is a blessing.

God's shingle is hung out to dry
from England's stony seaboard.
Seals clap praise, pulpit rocks pray
in tidal pools on Oregon's coast.
Holy grains are finely sifted
on Key West's stained-glass shores.
Sanctuary sands remain haven and port
at Hopetown in the Abacos.

And the Greek island margins
invoke memories of ancient sea gods.

THE MOTHER NAMES OF BEAR
Gwawdodyns (Welsh)

I am *Dea Artio*, whom Celts
Honored in Berne. My progeny knelt,
Accepting my fruits, food from vine and roots
To nourish their shiny bruin pelts.

Warrior-goddess is what Gauls called me,
Andarta (Strong Bear). Years they lived free,
The Alps at their backs, then Roman attacks.
Vicontii fought, filled with my *esprit*.

In the North, *Atla* was my name,
Scandinavian she-bear whose frame
Was sacred to Thor, in love and in war.
To battle fierce foes was ever our aim.

Many the titles the Christians took:
Ursula, Brigid are in *The Book
Of Saints*, but the truth (teach it to the youth)
Lies in my old goddess eyes, wild look.

I long to be at Brauron, where fair
Girls in yellow robes danced in prayers,
With animal pride, in powerful strides,
Honoring me, known simply as *Bear*.

TRANSAMPUTATION

The Great Mother is associated with the Great Bear in the heavens, with the number seven and the day of the week, Friday, when the fish sacrifice was made and eaten in her honour.
                                    -Encyclopedia of Traditional Symbols

"My foot's a fish."

That's what you said.

Filleted to bone, missing toes,

wrapped like any week-old sole

as they took you, piece by part

from the land

back out to sea,

my mermaid mother.

"Let's Go Mark!" Acrylic Wash by Mark Runge.

And What About Our Teddy Bear?

AND WHAT ABOUT OUR TEDDY BEAR?
Casbairdne (Irish)

Lore learned from lab animals:
(Scores discerned through wee weevil
brain scans, read by cerebral
meds, not vainly medieval).

That lore may look transcendent.
It isn't! Myths more elegant
spell scads of truths, *en passant*:
Dad's donkey, Mom's elephant,*

fat, spoiled cocker spaniel,
tan coiled cat—nine survivals—
Critter corps of maximal
lore learned from our animals.

---

*Dad was a lifelong Democrat, Mom a Republican.

A MADRIGAL BY AN UNNAMED BRUIN
Madrigal (Italian & English)

What will I say when I find my true love?
We go together, like teddy and bear,
All other furred arms I vow to forswear.

Let's be on a par, not below or above,
Let's live side by side, like table and chair.
What will I say when I find my true love?
We go together, like teddy and bear.

So if Bear, who'll smell like cinnamon clove,
Will cuddle with me in soft, secret lair,
Will meet my longings, and answer my prayer,
What will I say when I find my true love?
We go together, like teddy and bear,
All other furred arms I vow to forswear.

Lady Fern. Watercolor by Mark Runge.

LADY FERN AND THE THREE GREEN BEARS
(A Metrical Romance)

St. Ursula's Day is celebrated October 21. She is "the central figure of an important medieval cycle of tales in the Catholic Church. She received her bear name from defending her 11,000 virgins against the bear's onslaught. The true test of any saint's power, however, was not merely in overcoming the bear but in taming it."

-Shepard and Sanders, *The Sacred Paw*

I.

St. Ursula's Eve—and it was still hot—
A muggy Miami dusk made us droop.
We blamed the tropical heat and not the lot
Of merlot we'd drunk. We were a languid group
That night. You'd never know we used to troop
Off to battle each day, schoolteacher knights
Fighting ignorance that would keep kids dupes
Against our will . . . but enough of that! Right
Now we desultorily spoke—no great insights—

II.

I think I recall some chat about wars,
Who had citrus canker, who had angina,
And yes, I remember our looking at stars—
Now, where were Ursa Major and Minor?
I drowsed on our deck in the recliner
And listened as Sandra tied stars to the date—
(See, she's a Catholic, and owner
Of *The Oxford Dictionary of Saints*)
But then I heard a melody, first faint

III.
Then getting louder with each breath I took.
Plaintive and sweet, it arose from the shower.
No one else noticed, not a sign or a look
Of recognition, but when I heard "The flower
Of chivalry could not break down the tower
Love built," I knew I had heard this before.
Was it by that Frenchman or by John Gower?
Wasn't it "La Belle Dame Sans Merci," or . . .
Wait! "La Belle Ourse Sans Merci"—unrequited *l'amour!*

IV.
I must have gone to the door to espy
Who was minstreling this ancient ditty.
And maybe I glimpsed the shoe-button eye
Of my terry-cloth bear from Bed and Bath City,
But I'm sure I was drawn on by pretty
Loud voices emanating from the den.
Our clan of stuffed bears, all rather witty,
Live there, with some "others"—four not akin—
A mouse, cat, and dog, and a dwarf with acumen.

V.
Doc, the dwarf (from the Kingdom of Disney)
Was proclaimed "the judge" by bold Angel Cat,
Who directed Pooh Bear to blow (off key)
His herald's horn. With his ta-ta-ta-tat
Pooh quelled the noise. In his suave cravat,
Stuart Little organized bears in rows,
Except for Lady Fern, who'd stopped to chat
With Shirley Holmes Bear, who needs no intros.
I wondered what it meant, this strange scenario?

VI.

Their bruin lair, once familiar, now strange,
Made me shiver with curious insight.
The bear tent, which once seemed like "Home on the Range,"
Looked like a page from *The Arabian Nights*.
Its peaks were illumined by Christmas lights
Which shone with a newly exotic air.
"A bear's tent is his castle." Are those the right
Words to describe this enchanted affair?
I was to witness The Code of the Courtly Bear.

VII.

By that, I mean I saw bears with manners
Conduct a fair trial, with friends and some foes
Testifying. Some'd even made banners
Touting their champions. These all flew below
The Bear Nation's flag they'd hoisted, to show
Their united pride in the state of C A
Where Yosemite bears could prosper and grow . . .
But back to what happened next! The fey,
Straw-hatted Lady Fern, with Southern drawl, did say,

VIII.

"I'ah have been accused of be'in too chaste,
Of be'in bearly civil to these three
Cavaliers." She looked toward three bears, unplaced
Until now, who marched up with such *esprit*
That the crowd cheered and humphed with teddy bear glee
Until Doc shushed them, then frowned at Fern:
"Madam, you are not the appellée.
It's this trio that's of this court's concern.
Each green bear must speak.
Let's see what we learn."

IX.

The benches were crowded, wee bears in front
The better to see. Scuba Steve took off
His mask, Wee Dino his hood, but the blunt
Wee Chilly the Snowman refused to doff
His top-hat. Taco Dog began to woof.
Rosie (whose last name is Yogibeara)
Knocked a home run—the hat sailed aloft.
Fern weepily said (then fixed her mascara),
"This nev'ah would have happened back home at Tara."

X.

What quieted this hug, these combatant bears?
A voice rang out, "This is no tournament.
Why do you put on these martial airs?
We are here to have Fern make her judgment
Of who is more honest, brave, and eloquent."
The green bear who spoke raised his noble nose,
His beaded breastplate a rainbow adornment.
His Zulu chaplet love token revealed to those
Present that he was belovèd. I suppose

XI.

I must tell you, (sometimes he's too modest)
That he came from South Africa. His fame
Had preceded him. Stories of conquest
Were bandied about by bears whose acclaim
Of Nelson showed that they were of the same
Empire stock. His squires, Pooh Bear and Dunwell,
Had touted his honor, and cleared his name
Of rumors that linked him to Old Cornwall
Legends of Guinivbear and Bearcelot. Faithful

XII.

Compatriots hung on his every word.
I admit I dozed through his thrice-told tales
Of justice he'd sought for both smooth and furred,
Of Bearcelona where he'd found small grails
To bring back to this group. He gave details
Far beyond what we needed. Then, I swear,
The noise level rose twenty decibels.
The excitement centered on a new bear.
It was young, robust Greeley, in German mohair.

XIII.

Page Helmut called out, "He's Parziful's heir!"
Greeley shrugged off talk of his pedigree.
"It's true my maker, who birthed me with care,
Hails from Berlin. Her name is Gephardt, Bea.
But this is America, my country.
Yes, I do stunts, by myself, with no fuss,
On specially weighted legs, as you see.
My liege-bear and model? The bear made by Russ.
In *Chronicles** readings, I stand in for King Gus."

XIV.

You could tell the crowd loved Greeley a lot
For his fresh bright green brow, shaved way back,
For the innocence shining from eyes not
Yet jaded by dust and time. What was his tack
In his speech directed toward Fern? The lack
Of vigor in his older opponents.
Others had become his strong proponents.
Strength, charm, a knap-sack—he had all the components.

XV.

As partisan bears hurrahed for Greeley,
Baby Charlie from Stratford began to cry.
Fern rolled her eyes, but I knew she was really
Enjoying this mêlée. "Edify
Us!" She called to the third bear in green. "I'ah'd
Like to hear from Gus Greenbear, who started
This collection of bears. Please testify
As to your intentions. Your stout-hearted
Doubles may have rendered you loveless, outsmarted."

XVI.

Eddie (who's golden, not green in the least)
Sprang up and sputtered (he's more brawn than brains),
"All saints defend us—all bears, dwarves, and beasts!
Gus may be grizzled and suffer from stains,
But he's a great sport. His spirit sustains
His best buddies, like Wee Dino and me."
The rest of his fervent parley remains
Lost, for it was drowned out by banshee
Noises from the nightly flight of a parrot jamboree.

XVII.

But I caught most of Gus Greenbear's case,
Which he now made in his quiet and humble
Voice. "Yes, I am older," he said, a grimace
Marking his grey-green face, "and less noble.
I know Russ didn't sew me with a thimble
Of gold. I have climbed above my station."
Doc, who'd nodded off, cried, "Greenbear, don't mumble!"
Louder, more regally, Gus gave a summation
Of lessons he'd learned in his rough education:

Grizzled Gus. Watercolor by Mark Runge.

XVIII.

". . . so no one must have blue-threaded forebears
To be worthy, magnanimous, stately.
Remember his words, the great Shakesbear's?
'To thine own bear-self be true.' Fortunately,
I studied with Will, and ultimately . . . ."
Like the stuffed ones, I was falling asleep
As Gus orated on, then stopped, faintly
Alarmed as cubs, like leaves, snored in a heap . . .
Shirley Holmes blurted out, "You green bears must sew what you reap!"

XIX.

Doc said, "Step forward! Explain what you mean."
As you guessed, Miss Holmes was from Baker Street.
She was precise, pronouncing "been" like "bean,"
And cape and deerstalker cap were so neat.
Shirley hailed from the Scotland Yard elite.
But what did that have to do with romance?
With three smart green bears, the best you could meet?
She started, "I have some new facts." The glance
She shot Fern showed that this Sherlock was not hired by chance.

XX.

"You think these three bears pure in mind, fur, and soul?
And one most worthy of Fern's ursine love?
Dissuade yourselves of that rigmarole!"
The bears sat up straighter, like pines in a grove.
There were no giggles, no cut-ups, no shoves.
"First, let's take Nelson, who's really a spy
Called Double-O-One, and this I will prove,
And second, don't think that Greeley's your guy—
For thefts of Pooh's honey he has no alibi.

XXI.

As for Gus—yes, he's good—but still has flaws.
Just peek at his albums of photographs.
He's mugging in each—that should give you pause!
Chivalrous? Humble? Oh, don't make me laugh.
And what about girl bears (they're called 'distaff')?
Three out of twenty—and I'm one of those—
They let us make tea—and pass the carafe.
But the worst thing Gus did . . ." (all the bears froze)
"Was take in B.J., a pirate bear. Just suppose

XXII.

You were in Key West and met this scoundrel . . . ."
They all looked around, to glare at this scum,
But found just some notes, a parchment bundle.
Smart Shirley was surprised—even struck dumb—
For Fern was gone, too. The green bears looked numb
And bereft, for they'd lost Atlanta's prize.
Christmas Bear wept, and then began to drum
A sad beat. Before Doc could moralize
Too much, Dunwell, from London, said he'd scrutinize

XXIII.

The notes (for Brits can read maps and do accents),
And solve the mystery of sudden flight.
So here, in brief, were the papers' contents:
A treasure map (but no X marked, for spite)
And a short note from Fern (no, not contrite).
Seems she wrote, "B.J. is dashin', a real
Rhett type," and "Romance is a bruin's bearthright."
I forget some parts, those that were quite shrill,
But St. Ursula was on the parchment's red seal.

XXIV.

What time did they slip away? (Our friends
I mean, tired of wine and Beary Manilow.)
Sandra showed them out, as she often tends
To do when it's hot and the talk is slow.
Did the hug forget Miss Fern and her beau?
The baseball team is kinder to our Rosie—
They compliment her on her great fast throw.
Reality reigns, to a greater degree.
Like us, our bears seem happy to watch more TV.

*The adventures of Gus and his friends were first reported in *The Greenbear Chronicles*, as told to Sandra Riley by Gus Greenbear.

Lady Fern with the Three Green Bears: Greeley, Gus and Nelson.

THE RUBEARIYAT OF GUS GREENBEAR
WRITTEN BY SANDRA RILEY
ILLUSTRATED BY ERICK HERSHEY
Rubai (Arabic)

Afoot and light-hearted, I take to the open road, healthy, free, the world before me . . .
  - Walt Whitman, Song of the Open Road

Kiss a flower, deer-velvet soft.
Snuffle a fragrance, sun-soaked oft.
Look! There are hundreds more waiting.
No matter. I have all day off.

Open road and Big-Sky, riding
my Harley like a bird winging
through miles of golden wheat. No
honey-tree or berry-patch sighting?

Sea-weedy beach. No-see-ums grow.
In crystal water I wallow.
A starfish rests here by day. But
at night to the sky they all go.

Parrots squawk-talk to the sun. What
racket! We exchange scuttlebutt,
then settle down to quiet dreams
of huckleberries. (What's a pignut?)

Jumping, we spring off trampoline
like a Cirque Du Soleil twin-team,
catapault into the bamboo,
bears and trees arcing like star beams.

Dino Bear swings to the ground so-oo
smooth. I am swaying and flying too
high to jump down to the rocky earth.
'Tis a puzzlement! What to do?

On the ceiling of my cave berth
I draw art. Only a pennyworth
of candle left. When all the light
goes out, will these walls still be art?

On stage I stand in the limelight,
about to speak my speech just right
as Gentle Bear of Verona.
No sound or fury—just stage fright!

In the land of the Grand Pooh Bah
gold and gems wait. At siesta-
time, I rush to save Fern,
guarded by the dragon-fella.

Deep in the cavern, cauldrons burn.
Atop the treasure sits Lady Fern.
Dragon wakes. "Here, take the lady.
Her talk makes me crazy. Your turn!"

On mountain path I sing to trees.
All critters, even humble-bees
make sweet melodious music.
Why am I the one off-key?

"Mr. Caterpillar, I'm homesick
for my hug and our tent rustic."
"HOW MANY BEARS FIT IN THAT TENT?"
    "Well, there's . . . Eddie, Chilly, Rosie and Steve, Shirley, Greeley, Charley and Fern, Angel Cat, Taco Dog, Wee Dino and Doc, Dunwell, Nelson, Helmut and Pooh, White Bear, Stuart, B.J., and Ten-Ten when he comes to visit . . ."
"WAIT! CAN'T HAVE MORE BEARS THAN LEG-STICKS!"

I'm marching in a parade-event.
A flower falls by accident
from the Liberty-Bell float
onto my paw, not the pavement.

On Mississippi River boat
I spy a raft with Dino 'n goat.
"Ahoy! Is that a Goat Bear you haul?"
"I must carry him. He can't float."

By the big barn we play baseball.
Wee Dino Bear hits my fastball,
sends Rooster flapping from hayloft.
I think I'll take up basketball.

Yaay! I did it! No flowers left
to kiss. I nap in candy-tufts
and hear night frogs croak, "Kiss me!" I
must be dreaming or else gone daft.

"No flowers left to kiss."

Route 12, Idaho

ROUTE 12, IDAHO: THE LEWIS AND CLARK TRAIL
Edda Measures (Norse)

I myself have not o'erthrown thee … Thou thyself hast left the forest.
- Kalevala, Finnish

Soon after dawn we drove the Road,

West going east, easing homeward

Straight towards the sun. Sibilant lanes,

Lined thick with trees, took us beside

White, swift water, though way low this fall.

Mountains reared up, rose from the floor

Of lonely canyons that cradled our route:

Us, and the pines, the pavement—and bears.

A black shape ahead, absorbing the light

Startled and slowed us. We stopped on the road.

Manlike in gestures, gyrations and stance,

He stood in our path, proud bruin cub,

Recalling Norse notions, the legends

Of woolly heroes, only half men:

Bodvar Biarki (Bodvar Little
Bear) shifted his shape, could be
Human or bear. Not battle famous,
Bodvar safe kept the King, Hrolf of Denmark.

Protected by steel, silent and awed,
Two of us wistfully watched the wild dance
That our bear cub celebrated.
A sudden dash to the dark forest—
He was gone, guarding secrets.
Some bear magic? Mother nearby?
He'd come for bear claws I carry back home?
Did hunters harry him and his clan?
Or fires and farmlands force him to leave?
Somehow our questions quickened our pace.
Ten miles we sped, sprinting like deer,
When a second cub, charging the road,
Flashed so vividly, then vanished through brush.

[EXIT, pursued by a bear...]
-Shakespeare, *The Winter's Tale:* III, 3

ACKNOWLEDGMENTS

Poems in this work originally published elsewhere: "Glass Beach" in *RED OWL*, "What We Saw in Spokane, WA" in *EXIT 13*, "In Case of Bears" in *MÖBIUS*, "In Waste Places" in *POETRY OF THE PEOPLE*, "My Grandfather – Fred Clay Spradling" in *BIBLIOPHILOS*, "Morning Tea with Mount St. Helens" in *VQ ONLINE*, "Dreamcatcher Medicine" in *GOLDEN WORDS*, "Calamity Jane's Lament" on CITYOFDEADWOOD.COM, "At an Arts and Crafts Show in Pierce, Idaho" in *FROST NOTES* and *THE ANTHOLOGY OF NEW ENGLAND WRITERS*, "An Alarum, or Thereby Hangs a Tale" in *THEMA*, and "Sylvia's Prayer" in *POETS AT WORK*.

Photograph on page 100 by EDWARD S. CURTIS, reprinted by kind permission of the McCormick Library of Special Collections, Northwestern University. Cover painting, paintings on pages 23, 25, 118 and woodwork on page 111 by BEVERLY FROST. Paintings on pages 108, 124, 128 and 135 by MARK RUNGE. Illustrations on pages 140 to 143 by ERICK HERSHEY. Mural paintings on pages 96, 98, 106 by MARIA SOLIDAY. Photograph on page 96 by JACK LAMONT. Photographs on pages 112 and 148 by FRANK WENDELN (photo, page 112 originally appeared in *Gus 'n Us* by Peggy C. Hall ©1999). Additional photography by PEGGY C. HALL, SANDRA RILEY, and JASON STOETZER.

I am grateful to all those teachers, students, and friends who listened and applauded even when I *didn't* make blueberry muffins. Well, there's ... SANDY, CECY, SYLVIA and FRANK, JACKIE, TRAVIS, CHRISSY and STEVE, TAMARA, ELLEN, HAROLD and GWEN, ROME, SUZY, CATHI and GAIL, JASON, MARK, MEL and ELVIRA, and DAVID, when he comes to visit ...

INDEX OF FORMS

NAME OF FORM	ORIGIN	USED IN POEM	PAGE
Ae Freislighe	IRISH	"Getting Our Bearings"	19
Antiphon	liturgical	"Antiphon, with Drums"	114
Awdl Gywydd	WELSH	"The Collection"	110
Bob & Wheel	ENGLISH	"An Alarum, or Thereby Hangs a Tale"	82
Byr A Thoddaid	WELSH	"A Wild Quadrille"	104
Canzone	ITALIAN	"In Case of Bears"	20
Casbairdne	IRISH	"And What About Our Teddy Bear?"	126
Clogyrnach	WELSH	"My Grandfather – Fred Clay Spradling"	92
Cyhydedd Hir	WELSH	"You Gotta Have Art"	107
Cyhydedd Naw Ban	WELSH	"On the Rocks"	99
Cyrch A Chwta	WELSH	"All is Fair…"	88
Cywydd Deuair Hirion	WELSH	"The Players at Silver Springs, Florida"	18
Cywydd Llosgyrnog	WELSH	"Frank's Prayer"	42
Deibhidhe	IRISH	"Lullaby, My Baby Bear"	94
Dizain	FRENCH	"For Sylvia, Our Spider Woman"	40
Droighneach	IRISH	"For Frank, the Man Who Sees Animals"	43
Edda Measures	NORSE	"Route 12, Idaho"	146
Elegiacs	GREEK	"An Old Feud"	65
Englyn Unodl Crwca	WELSH	"On Whiskey Creek"	84
Epistle	didactics	"An Epistle from Idaho to Maria, in Miami, Florida"	49
Glose	SPANISH & PORTUGUESE	"A Glose on Roethke's 'In a Dark Time'"	86
Gwawdodyns	WELSH	"The Mother Names of Bear"	122
Haiku	JAPANESE	"The Redwoods Reign"	75
Hir A Thoddaid	WELSH	"CeleBEARations"	117
Kyrielle	FRENCH	"It's Like …"	16
Lai	FRENCH	"My Birthday in Three Steps"	119
Lai Nouveau	FRENCH	"My Birthday in Three Steps"	119
Madrigal	ITALIAN & ENGLISH	"A Madrigal by an Unnamed Bruin"	127
Pantoum	MALAYAN	"A Pantoum for Mark Runge"	109
Rannaigheacht Mhór	IRISH	"Irish, Indeed"	89
Rhupunt	WELSH	"Badgers and Bears"	83
Rionnaird Tri-Nard	IRISH	"To Teddy Roosevelt"	85
Romance	FRENCH	"Lady Fern and the Three Green Bears"	129
Rubai	ARABIC	"The Rubeariyat of Gus Greenbear"	140
Séadna	IRISH	"Brother Bear"	90
Sneadhbhairdne	IRISH	"Saturday Matinée"	105
Standard *Habbie*	SCOTTISH	"On Taking Chances in Idaho"	50
Triversen	AMERICAN	"Idaho Morning"	34
Virelai	FRENCH	"My Birthday in Three Steps"	119

A NOTE ON TYPEFACES

This book has been set in four fonts, two of which are relevant to the bear themes: URSA, created by Jim Pearson, for poetic form names, cover text and section titles, and BEARPAW, created by Dennis Anderson, for poem titles. The forms named in "My Birthday in Three Steps" were set in KRAZYKOOL.

In honor of the late comedienne Lady Zelma Bulmer, the primary text has been set in the BULMER font. All fonts are registered shareware and freely available online.

www.ingramcontent.com/pod-product-compliance
Lightning Source LLC
Chambersburg PA
CBHW020905090426
42736CB00008B/507